SECRETS
of
THE VINE

❧ LEADER'S GUIDE ❧

BRUCE
WILKINSON

Dear friend,

The longer I live, the truer this idea seems: the purpose of life is to be fruitful. If you're like me, you come to those moments in life when you find yourself asking, "How will the world be different for my having lived in it? What will I leave behind as a legacy? What am I doing that really counts?"

Secrets of the Vine, as you may already know, is all about the answers to those questions. Perhaps you've read our little book; perhaps you've already begun to see your life differently as a result. If so, you can see that the group experience you are about to lead is one more opportunity to bear lovely, abundant fruit for Jesus. For your guidance in this video experience will have a tremendous impact on the life-change that occurs in your participants.

That's why you'll want to study this leader's guide, as well as the student's edition, very closely before each session. You'll want to prayerfully prepare the most dynamic sessions possible. Then, my friend, you can take the lead in fruit-bearing—and someday God will look at your group members, smile back at you, and say, "Well done! This is the fruit I was looking for."

Yours in joyful abundance,

Bruce Wilkinson

Bruce Wilkinson
Author, *The Prayer of Jabez*
and *Secrets of the Vine*

Project Director: Dorit Radandt; Design: Lois Gable;
Editor: Rob Suggs; Cover illustration by Katia Andreeva

TABLE
of CONTENTS

LEADING THE SECRETS OF THE VINE VIDEO SERIES

Are you ready to bear fruit? Dr. Bruce Wilkinson's best-selling book *Secrets of the Vine* takes up where *The Prayer of Jabez* left off, with the question of how we can expand our boundaries (that is, bear fruit) in life to please God. Now you have the opportunity to help your group explore the most effective ways to do that. This Leader's Guide will walk you through all the steps to help make your experience unforgettable.

How Are The Sessions Designed?

Secrets of the Vine will offer four sessions. The series includes two video sessions of approximately 30 minutes for each portion.

We've also included a third, non-video session for each section as an option to consider—a group discovery session to move your people deeper into the Prayer. You might consider:

- **The Express Study:** 4 sessions—two video viewings in each.
- **The Standard Study:** 8 sessions, all video.
- **The Expanded Study:** 12 sessions including four group discovery sessions.

	Express (4 weeks)		Standard (8 weeks)		Expanded (12 weeks)
1	Fruit-Bearing	1	Fruit-Bearing A (video)	1	Fruit-Bearing A (video)
	A and B (video)	2	Fruit-Bearing B (video)	2	Fruit-Bearing B (video)
				3	Fruit-Bearing (group)
2	"No Fruit" to "Fruit"	3	"No Fruit" to "Fruit" A (video)	4	"No Fruit" to "Fruit" A (video)
	A & B (video)	4	"No Fruit" to "Fruit" B (video)	5	"No Fruit" to "Fruit" B (video)
				6	"No Fruit" to "Fruit" (group)
3	"Fruit" to "More Fruit"	5	"Fruit" to "More Fruit" A (video)	7	"Fruit" to "More Fruit" A (video)
	A & B (video)	6	"Fruit" to "More Fruit" B (video)	8	"Fruit" to "More Fruit" B (video)
				9	"Fruit" to "More Fruit" (group)
4	"More Fruit" to "Much Fruit"	7	"More Fruit" to "Much Fruit" A (video)	10	"More Fruit" to "Much Fruit" A (video)
	A & B (video)	8	"More Fruit" to "Much Fruit" B (video)	11	"More Fruit" to "Much Fruit" B (video)
				12	"More Fruit" to "Much Fruit" (group)

LEADING THE SESSIONS

First and foremost, expect the Lord to do great things through your sessions together! None of your attendees come by chance—they are here by divine appointment to discover how their lives can be more fruitful, more abundant, and more eternally significant. Pray for your people each day in preparation for *Secrets of the Vine*. Expect God to begin using the Secrets in you by bearing fruit through each individual who attends your sessions.

You'll need to consider three major objectives as you prepare:

1. Choosing a time, place and format for holding the sessions.

2. Making arrangements for location and logistics.

3. Actively promoting and encouraging attendance.

4. Praying and preparing spiritually.

5. Leading successful sessions.

The following pages will offer some practical, helpful tips to make you an effective leader. But there's room for flexibility. Apply these guidelines to the specific situation of your group, whether in the classroom of a church, the home of a friend, or the conference room of an office.

Choosing the Schedule and Format

- **Study the chart on the preceding page.** What kind of format will best meet your group's needs—the quick four-session "Express," the eight-session "Standard" or the full, deluxe 12-session "Expanded" study? Decide which is best for your group and situation.

- **Plan the wisest use of time.** Video sessions last approximately 30 minutes, but your group time is a variable. Adapt our activity suggestions to fit your balance of time. Advance preparation on your part is essential.

Decide in advance how much time you want to give to each question and each activity.

LEADING
THE SESSIONS

2

For the Sunday School Class

2 months before the sessions. Call and write class members. Carefully explain the series and its purpose. Begin building excitement by spreading the word through the church.

1 month before the sessions. Meet with your team to pray and plan. Use posters, flyers, and bulletin inserts to spread the word.

2 weeks before the sessions. Contact members again. Make a list of details to check, including room availability, a good VCR and monitor, workbooks, etc. Spend extra time in daily prayer.

For the Home Group

1 month before the sessions. Call and write group members. Ask them to consider bringing a friend. Begin talking consistently and excitedly about the series.

2 weeks before the sessions. Discuss the importance of the series with your members. Check VCR, materials, etc. Send out cards inviting friends to your group. Pray daily.

For the Church or Large Group Format

3 months before the sessions. Write key church or organizational leaders. Provide information to them. Use posters, flyers, and local advertising to promote your seminar.

2 months before the sessions. At church, begin promoting the seminars from the pulpit during worship. Check course materials, room availability, refreshment plans, other logistics. Delegate jobs to workers—greeting, refreshments, follow-up, etc.

1 week before the sessions. Plan a final phone blitz. Make final checks on logistics. Use signs and be sure visitors can find the room. Schedule a special prayer meeting.

3 Maximize Session Time

Create an effective learning environment.

Arrange the room. Are the chairs in the best place for viewing the video? Is the monitor set up to avoid window glare? For large groups, procure a video projector or large-screen television.

Name tags are always a good idea. Provide tags and bold pens. Arrange for a friendly host or hostess to greet people as they arrive. Provide extra pencils for note-taking.

Refreshments help the fellowship factor and build a comfortable and responsive group. Have light refreshments before or after your meeting as it suits your particular arrangement.

Prepare for the Session.

Pray with focus—before, during and after the seminars. Pray for specific participants. Nothing you do in preparation will be more important.

Know the content. Go over the video and notebook material. Anticipate likely questions.

Be transformed by the material, and be prepared to share how the secrets of fruitfulness have impacted your life.

Keep it moving without rushing.

Balance time management with sensitive group dynamics. Cover the material, but be flexible enough to deal with your group's needs as the Spirit leads you.

Don't be sidetracked. If it a member's question is complex, handle it after the session or privately during the week. Keep the whole group in mind.

Be personable and responsive.

Know names! Keep a list of participants, make notes and review during the week. Greet people by name; it makes a difference

Build group chemistry. Help people interact and get to know each other.

PERSONALIZE YOUR SESSION

- **One-Hour Sessions.** If you use a 60-minute format, you'll have slightly less than 30 minutes for the balance of activities after the video. Carefully guide the interaction. Encourage people to arrive early. Delay prayer requests and announcements for the final moments. Use questions that encourage short answers. Use small group time, dividing quickly and providing one key question for discussion. See the chart below.

- **Ninety minutes or longer.** Lengthier sessions provide greater flexibility. You'll be able to build more quality and depth into small group times. You'll also have more time available for questions, deeper topic exploration, and prayer. See the chart below.

- **Optional Workshop Weeks.** This book includes material for extra sessions for each of the four Secrets. The workshop session would use no video but devote the time to group interaction. This is strongly recommended if time permits.

Time Allotments for 60- and 90-Minute Sessions and the Express Study

	For One-Hour Session...	For a 90-Minute Session...	For a 4-week Express Study...
Introduce the session.	5 minutes total	15 minutes total	5 minutes total
• Greet the group.	2 minutes	5 minutes	2 minutes
• Introduce the video.	3 minutes	5 minutes	3 minutes
• Build the need.	------------	5 minutes	------------
Play the Video.	**Allow 30 minutes.**	**Allow 30 minutes.**	**Allow 60 minutes.**
Interact with the group.	**20 minutes total**	**40 minutes total**	**20 minutes total**
• Summarize the "Big Idea."	2 minutes	3 minutes	2 minutes
• Question and answer.	6 minutes	8 minutes	6 minutes
• Interaction in smaller groups.	6 minutes	20 minutes	6 minutes
• Give a homework assignment.	1 minutes	1 minutes	1 minutes
• Prayer time.	5 minutes	8 minutes	5 minutes

FRUIT-BEARING

1. Introduce the session

• **Launch the session.** Greet everyone enthusiastically. Ask one or two participants to share what they're hoping to accomplish through this study.

• **Introduce the material.** Ask: "Do you think God has one central purpose for your life? Several? Have you ever considered what these may be?" Allow a moment for reflection.

• **Build the need.** Say: "Through this study you will discover the greatest things God wants to accomplish through your life— and you will find out secrets of bearing more fruit for Him."

2. Play the Video (Course Workbook pages 12-14)

Allow 30 minutes for Dr. Wilkinson's video presentation. Make sure the volume is sufficient, and that everyone has a good view.

Watch for the Big Idea: This session presents an overview of the *Secrets of the Vine.* Make sure your people catch the insight that every single person is in one of the four baskets described by Dr. Wilkinson—and God wants all of us to be in the fourth basket ("much fruit").

When the video has concluded, ask for questions and comments. Some will ask which words go in certain blanks. Attend to these questions clearly. Launch into your discussion without delay.

3. Guide the Discussion

Note: Leaders should adapt this material to fit the time available.
Consult the first section of this book for time allotments. These first two questions are for the entire group.

1. What was the single most significant, life-changing idea you heard in this presentation?

2. What did you realize about your own life as you considered these ideas?

Divide the group into units of two or three. Direct them to the discussion questions on page 15 of the video workbook. Included on this page are comments you can use as you lead the discussion.

Question 1. This question requires a review of the most important points from the first session. Be certain each person is clear on each portion of the fruit-bearing process—how the vinedresser (God) brings fruit through the branches of the vine.

Question 2. Good works are the fruit of faith, for true belief changes the way we behave. As James teaches, it is impossible to know God without serving Him through our works.

Question 3. Fruit is a good work done with a God-honoring motive and is pleasing to God. When we are not living to please God, even as believers, we are not bearing fruit.

Question 4. The resolution is to work in partnership with God. If we leave it all to God, or try to do it all on our own, no fruit will result. We are responsible through the power God gives us.

Question 5. This is the most important question of all, and your group members should be given a few moments to consider the answer. This will lead into the homework assignment, where this question will be personally worked out in more detail.

Homework: Work with pen and paper. Based on your analysis of the use of your time and talents, identify the actual current focus of your life as indicated by those factors. Then write what you feel God would like your focus to be. How will you make that come true?

FRUIT-BEARING

1. Introduce the Session

• **Greet the group.** Welcome everyone back to a new session. Briefly review the Big Idea from last week and describe how it affected your life during the week.

• **Introduce the concept.** *Ask:* "Have you ever wondered how many different ways one person can change the world? What are the 'widest'? What are the 'deepest'?"

• **Build the need.** *Ask:* "What if you knew exactly how you could bear the most fruit in life, and you knew which areas were the most important? By the time we finish this session, you'll be able to answer both questions."

2. Play the Video (Course Workbook pages 16-18)

Allow 30 minutes for the video presentation. Check the player, the volume, and the visibility for the whole group.

Watch for the Big Idea: God gives us special areas in which to bear fruit abundantly. This brings great delight not only to God but to us as well.

3. Guide the Discussion

Before this week's session, evaluate the effectiveness of the previous session. Was there enough time? Did you get bogged down somewhere? Reflect and adjust. Use these first two questions with the entire group, then divide into smaller units for questions on the following page.

1. In what ways did today's presentation change your idea of fruit-bearing?

2. What type of fruit-bearing excites and intrigues you the most? Why?

Divide the group into units of two or three. Direct them to the discussion questions on page 19 of the video workbook. Use the following comments to help you explore the questions.

Question 1. Much of what people do in life is done in private. We receive little or no picture of the fruit someone bears in family life, and we judge only from what is visible and public—suggesting that we should not be judging the fruit of others, only our own.

Question 2. This question should help your group members cultivate a deeper appreciation for those services and ministries provided publicly by the church. Be sure to encourage them to be certain they are involved in these ministries, which are our responsibility in fruit-bearing.

Question 3. Your group members are likely to have already given this some thought as they viewed the video. Allow them to share their responses with the group and encourage each other toward these goals. Each person should be able to give at least one answer that excites them.

Question 4. This question reminds us that it's our responsibility not only to bear fruit, but to "stir up love and good works" in others. This group is a good forum for doing that. Look over the two Scriptural passages closely and suggest ways to help each other bear this kind of fruit.

Question 5. This question is a good barometer for measuring the fruit we are already bearing. If we are doing so, there are people who would be impacted by losing us. Suggestion: Rather than discuss this question, have a time of prayer in which each member can consider the answer and ask God to help them make a greater impact in fruit-bearing.

Homework: Think of all the things you do, and list every possible current channel for fruit-bearing in your life. Rank them in terms of how you feel they please God, and also in terms of how effectively and fruitfully you feel that you accomplish them.

GROUP INTERACTION

FRUIT-BEARING

Optional Bible Study Session

If you'd like to go deeper into God's Word with each of the four Secrets, you can devote an entire session to working as a group to explore the Bible passage below.

Leader's Checklist

☐ I've fervently prayed for this session.

☐ I've thoroughly planned for this session.

☐ I've thoughtfully pondered the concepts.

☐ I've personally practiced the concepts.

1. Introduce the Session

• **Greet the group.** Explain that this session is devoted to interacting with Scripture. There is no video presentation, but a great opportunity to taste the abundant fruit of God's Word.

• **Build the need.** *Ask:* "Do you feel the gentle prodding of the Lord, urging you to take a much closer look at the fruit you should be bearing in life? Would you like to "move to the next basket"? Today you can make it happen."

2. Divide into small groups

• Place your members in units of three or four members each. These groups will be retained for all four Group Discovery sessions.

• Pray for everyone. Ask God's Spirit to guide each group into exciting discoveries.

3. Reviewing the Secrets

• Move quickly through the main points of the first two sessions. Some may have missed one or even both sessions. Review both sessions over a few minutes.

4. Fruit Inspection: What's in Your Basket?

Which category describes your fruit-bearing? Discuss your "basket" with the group.

1—I'm in the empty basket—no fruit.

2—I'm in the second basket—fruit.

3—I'm in the third basket—more fruit.

4—I'm in the fourth basket—much fruit.

5. Discovering the Word: Fruit-Bearing

Read John 15:1-8 together. *This is the basic package for the* Secrets of the Vine. *Discuss these questions, making use of the hints in parentheses.*

1. Why do you think Jesus chose this particular word picture? What is the most effective part of the symbolism of the vinedresser, the vine, the branches, and the fruit? *(Leader: Use this question to help your group members thoroughly examine the central ideas of the Vine.)*

2. A branch grows out of a vine. How is this true with believers and Christ? *(We must be just as dependent upon Him for our "sap," or power in life. Without being connected to Him, we can bear no fruit in life.)*

3. Jesus saved this teaching for almost the last moment of the time He would be with His disciples. Why do you think He did this? What does it imply for your life? *(Tremendous importance is implied for this teaching. This is the basic command Jesus has given us, and the one by which we are to be evaluated.)* in midst of disappointment, fear, disillussn

4. What factors in your life have led to you being in the "basket" that you now identify as your fruit-bearing status? What factors would lead to an upgrade? *(See preceding page. Each group member should already have made this evaluation.)*

5. What specific action can you take this week to place fruit-bearing closer to the center of your life? Who will hold you accountable to doing this? *(Allow each group member to share his or her answer, and make plans to check on and encourage each other.)*

6. Praying Together

Leave sufficient time for group prayer at the end of your session. Group members should seek God's power toward a breakthrough in bearing more fruit for Him. Be sure to praise and thank God for His awesome goodness and lovingkindness. As the leader, call on God to perform miracles in the lives of your group members.

Homework: Tell your group that next week reveals the first secret of fruit-bearing. Ask them to come ready to report on their progress in seeing their lives more focused on that task.

SECRET #1:
"NO FRUIT" TO "FRUIT"

Leader's Checklist

☐ I've fervently prayed for this session.

☐ I've thoroughly planned for this session.

☐ I've thoughtfully pondered the concepts.

☐ I've personally practiced the concepts.

1. Introduce the Session

• **Launch the session.** Welcome everyone to the second part of *Secrets of the Vine*. Ask if anyone would like to share a breakthrough that was made through the homework assignment.

• **Introduce the material.** *Ask:* "Have you ever wondered how God feels about those who never bear fruit? Have you wondered what He does? The answer will surprise you!"

• **Build the need.** *Ask:* "What if you could walk away from this session and immediately eliminate a great deal of the pain and frustration that always seems to be with you? Today you'll see it in a completely new way, and you'll know what to do about it."

2. Play the Video (Course Workbook pages 26-28)

Allow 30 minutes for Dr. Wilkinson's video presentation.

Watch for the Big Idea: So much pain and frustration comes in our lives because God is disciplining us with various levels of severity, based on how stubbornly we refuse to bear fruit. This is a loving discipline—but it can be very difficult nonetheless.

When the video has concluded, ask your people to name the three stages of discipline. Make certain everyone followed the key insights of this presentation, then use the following general questions with the whole group.

3. Guide the Discussion

Always take a moment for review, connecting the last session's insight to this week's insight.

1. What was the most surprising thing you learned about God's discipline today? How do you respond emotionally to such an idea?

2. How has your view of fruit-bearing changed as a result of today's teaching?

Divide the group into units of two or three. Direct them to the discussion questions on page 29 of the student workbook. Included on this page are comments you can use as you lead the discussion.

Question 1.   It is important for us to understand that God disciplines as a loving Father—using "tough love" where necessary, but always trying to bring us to a position of fruit-bearing that will bring joy to us and to Him.

Question 2.   Note that "take away" actually means "lift up." Review how a vinedresser does this for those branches that trail in the dust. We see love and nurture rather than anger and punishment.

Question 3.   The purpose is to break our pattern of choosing to live fruitlessly. And He disciplines at various levels according to the extent of our disobedience.

Question 4.   There is a fear, but not a fear based in God's anger—rather in the necessary consequences to our own rebellion and disobedience. As long as we understand the truth of God as the loving gardener, we are motivated not only to avoid pain but to please Him and ourselves.

Question 5.   A powerful insight: In responding to discipline the right way, we not only bear fruit but attain a measure of holiness. This certainly motivates us to accept God's discipline and begin bearing the fruit He wants us to bear. Again, we ultimately bring joy not only to ourselves but to God.

Homework: At home, write out the three levels of God's discipline and identify one period when you experienced it—and why. Where are you now? If you are experiencing any form of God's discipline at the present, place a star next to that one. How do you plan to respond? Be specific.

SECRET #1:
"NO FRUIT" TO "FRUIT"

1. Introduce the Session

• **Launch the session.** We are exploring the first *Secret of the Vine:* how to move from fruitlessness to fruit-bearing. Mention the levels of discipline and ask for hands or nods of the head for everyone who dealt with this issue over the last few days.

• **Introduce the material.** *Say:* "Think of a time from childhood when you were punished for disobedience. No one enjoys it, but when discipline is lovingly applied, it should move us to become wiser and more productive."

• **Build the need.** *Ask:* "Wouldn't you like to move from the pain of disobeying God to the world of joy in bearing fruit? Today we will learn more about victory in accepting God's discipline."

2. Play the Video (Course Workbook pages 30-32)

Allow 30 minutes for Dr. Wilkinson's video presentation.

Watch for the Big Idea: Self-judgment and personal discipline help us avoid the pain of God applying discipline. There is hope in the realization that we are in control of how much of this painful process we must experience.

When the video has concluded, ask your group members to name the three methods of judging ourselves. Then use the following questions to explore these truths in more depth.

3. Guide the Discussion

Always take a moment for review, connecting the last session's insight to this week's insight.

1. Today we learned more about discipline, yet most of us probably found this presentation encouraging rather than discouraging. Why is that?

2. How much pain in life do you think might be avoided if we appropriately judged and disciplined ourselves? Why?

Divide the group into units of two or three. Direct them to the discussion questions on page 33 of the student workbook. Here are some key insights to the questions.

Question 1.   The classic misconception is to assume that all misfortune comes from the devil when, in fact, we may be observing God's severe discipline in the life of someone living in disobedience. We should react by lovingly helping the sufferer determine the true cause.

Question 2.   Sometimes we are reluctant to accept that God disciplines, but we understand the principle much more readily when we examine the place of parental discipline in our own lives.

Question 3.   This is a shocking insight for many of us: God disciplines unforgiveness as severely as sexual immorality. The truth is that unforgiveness is even more universal. No group member should leave this session without reflecting upon his or her own lack of forgiveness.

Question 4.   Be sure to review both psalms closely and to note the emotions of David. We are reassured when we observe the level of joy and rejuvenation that David experienced simply because he accepted God's discipline.

Question 5.   Will your group members be transparent enough to share such personal issues? Be gentle and be certain they're comfortable in sharing. The rewards of group prayer and encouragement make the pain of honesty worthwhile.

Homework: Identify the most glaring sin in your life. Write a plan for dealing with it using these three steps: Repentance, Restoration, Reconciliation. Examine the meaning of each word carefully, then note what each will demand from your life. Pray over this exercise.

SECRET #1:
"NO FRUIT" TO "FRUIT"

Optional Bible Study Session

*Go deeper into the Secrets with this group workshop session to
help you explore the Bible passage below.*

Leader's Checklist

☐ I've fervently prayed for this session.

☐ I've thoroughly planned for this session.

☐ I've thoughtfully pondered the concepts.

☐ I've personally practiced the concepts.

1. Introduce the Session

• **Greet the group.** Remind your group that this session is devoted to interacting with Scripture. There is no video presentation, but plenty of time to work together.

• **Build the need.** *Ask:* "How was your week? Do you feel you're bearing almost no fruit for God? How would you like to move to the next level? We'll work on that today."

2. Divide into small groups

• Place your members in units of three or four members each.

• Pray for everyone. Ask God's Spirit to guide each group into exciting discoveries.

3. Reviewing the Secrets

• Move quickly through the main points of the Secret #1. Some may have missed one or even both sessions. Review both sessions over a few minutes.

4. Discipline: Where Are You?

Which category describes your position in relation to God's discipline?

1—I'm bearing fruit for God! I detect no discipline at all.

2—I'm feeling His rebuke. Things aren't quite right.

3—I'm being chastened, and I feel considerable pain.

4—I'm experiencing scourging, and my life is in chaos.

5—I'm unsure about my status. I'm here to find out!

5. Discovering the Word: "No Fruit" to "Fruit"

Read Hebrews 12:5-11. *This is a central New Testament passage on discipline. Discuss these questions, making use of the hints in parentheses.*

1. How does it help to understand God's discipline as being like that of a parent? In what ways do the two compare? How are they different? *(Most of us understand parental discipline, so it helps us accept what God imposes. Their forms are similar in their increasing degrees, designed to teach us correct behavior. They differ because God is the only perfect Parent.)*

2. Whom does God discipline, according to verse 6? How does that change our understanding? *(We know that discipline is a proof of His love, just as it is in the case of effective parents.)*

3. According to verse 10, what is the result of discipline? What would this mean for your life? *(We become partakers of His holiness, a wonderful incentive. That will mean a stronger and wiser character, more like God, in every respect. Encourage participants to share what will be different about their lives.)*

4. How exactly does discipline produce more fruit in us (verse 11)? *("The peaceable fruit of righteousness" comes from us changing our ways to bring them in conformance to what God wants us to do. Our lives then become fruitful because we are different people.)*

5. Discuss where you see yourself right now in regard to God's discipline. What evidence is there? How will you respond this week? *(Allow plenty of time for group members to answer this question, preferably one-on-one with another group member. They check up during the next few days and encourage each other.)*

6. Praying Together

Leave sufficient time for group prayer at the end of your session. Praise and thank God. Reflect with Him on the wonderful truth of His perfect plan and discipline as our Father in heaven. Ask Him to show each one of us where we are in His ways of discipline, and how we should respond this week. Allow a moment for silent meditation, as each group member reflects on his or her own personal situation.

Homework: Spend each day working on your response to God's prodding to bear fruit in the way He is leading you to do. Note the changes this makes in your behavior, and the improvement in your fellowship with Him.

SECRET #2:
"FRUIT" TO "MORE FRUIT"

1. Introduce the Session

<table>
<tr><td>

Leader's Checklist

☐ I've fervently prayed
for this session.

☐ I've thoroughly planned
for this session.

☐ I've thoughtfully
pondered the concepts.

☐ I've personally practiced
the concepts.

</td></tr>
</table>

• **Launch the session.** Welcome everyone to the third section of *Secrets of the Vine*. Allow someone to share the life-change they've experienced since this series began.

• **Introduce the material.** *Say:* "Many of us are bearing some fruit for God, but we never move forward. We get stuck and feel discouragement because we don't bear more. There is something God does to help us move to that next level."

• **Build the need.** *Ask:* "Remember how you felt when you broke through to a new level in work or play? It feels great! How'd you like to feel the exhilaration of breaking through to more fruit for God—can you imagine the joy He would give you? Let's find out how."

2. Play the Video (Course Workbook pages 40-42)

Allow 30 minutes for Dr. Wilkinson's video presentation.

Watch for the Big Idea: Pruning is the process by which God gives us more capacity for fruit-bearing, but it can be painful—and feel like discipline. To cooperate with God in pruning, we must understand what it is, and what changes it will bring in our lives.

When the video has concluded, ask your people to name the three pruning principles. Make certain everyone followed the key insights of this presentation, then use the following general questions with the whole group.

3. Guide the Discussion

Always take a moment for review, connecting the last session's insight to this week's insight.

1. *Ask:* "How many of you have been pruned by God without realizing it? How do you feel about that now?"

2. How much more or less do you expect to enjoy your life if you cooperate with God in pruning? Why?

Divide the group into units of two or three. Direct them to the discussion questions on page 43 of the student workbook. Here are some comments to help you with each question.

Question 1.   Ask this question, then use the chart on page 21 if needed. These three concepts give the broad perspective to what is happening when God does the pruning in our lives.

Question 2.   Each group member, if he or she considers carefully, will be able to remember a time when they felt a pain—"but it was a good pain." The pain is "good" when we know God is helping us bear more fruit. Ask for examples that show pruning as opposed to discipline.

Question 3.   Take the time to examine each of these scenarios. Your group should see that each of these three "p" words is an essential area in which pruning must occur. Encourage your group members to imagine a life with the right priorities, purpose, and passion.

Question 4.   Ask which of the three examples above most reminds each member of himself or herself. This is a highly significant question, so give it a few minutes. You might allow each member to share with a partner and pray together.

Question 5.   Here is an opportunity for personal conviction and fresh commitment. You might arrange to have a time of dedication based on this question.

Homework: List the three pruning principles on a sheet of paper. Then spend time reflecting and writing upon the subject of where you are in each. Give yourself a numerical estimate from 0 to 10. Are your priorities where they should be? Are you passionate enough? Are you focused on a purpose? This should be a life-transforming exercise.

SECRET #2:
"FRUIT" TO "MORE FRUIT"

1. Introduce the Session

• **Launch the session.** After greeting everyone, explain that we are in the midst of the second secret of fruit-bearing. Briefly review the three pruning principles from the previous session.

• **Introduce the material.** *Say:* "Life has a way of dealing with us when we become too busy, doesn't it? The truth is that it is God who deals with us—and He does it through pruning."

• **Build the need.** *Ask:* "Do you feel burdened today, feeling that life has become too complex? What if you could find the way to rest and release that burden in the realization of how God was working in you? In this session you'll find out how to do that."

2. Play the Video (Course Workbook pages 44-47)

Allow 30 minutes for Dr. Wilkinson's video presentation.

Watch for the Big Idea: There are many ways and many areas where God will prune us. He does it throughout our lives, and if we recognize His pruning shears at work, we can be joyful instead of frustrated.

When the video has concluded, ask your group members to tell the most surprising truth they've learned about pruning. Use the two questions below to get them talking.

3. Guide the Discussion.

Always take a moment for review, connecting the last session's insight to this week's insight.

1. We discussed several ways God is perfect in the ways He prunes us. Which do you find the most reassuring? Why?

2. Pruning goes on throughout life. Does this encourage or discourage you? Why?

Divide the group into units of two or three. Direct them to the discussion questions on page 48 of the student workbook. Here are some key insights to the questions.

Question 1.   In the course of a lifetime, we will experience all or most of the pruning tools of God. It's helpful to carefully observe them in the life of Joseph so that we will be prepared.

Question 2.   This is a personal question that will require some reflection, though your group members have probably begun thinking about it during the video. Ask if someone would like to share their situation, and allow group members to encourage and pray for that member.

Question 3.   Pruning involves cutting away the non-essential—the things that take all the "sap" or energy we need for fruit-bearing. For us, this usually means activities and relationships that don't further God's purposes (or, whether we realize it or not, our own). It's painful to cut out little bits of life, but in time we see the wisdom of it.

Question 4.   The call for sacrifice is challenging. Help each group member honestly face the sacrifices they feel God is calling them to make. You might have them write it down privately on paper first, but encourage people to share with the group. The "more" refers to fruit, of course. As we think about sacrifice, it helps to also think about more fruit that will result.

Question 5.   Some people may never have articulated a life purpose. Ask your people to use the suggestions offered within this question to begin thinking about a life purpose. This will carry over into the week's homework assignment.

Homework: Continue thinking and praying daily about your life purpose. Write out your thoughts about it through the week, and ask God to help you clarify that purpose, as you cooperate with Him in the pruning process that will help you bear more fruit toward it.

SECRET #2:
"FRUIT" TO "MORE FRUIT"

Optional Session / Group Session

*Hold a workshop session to dig deeper in the subject
of being more fruit for God.*

Leader's Checklist

- ☐ I've fervently prayed for this session.
- ☐ I've thoroughly planned for this session.
- ☐ I've thoughtfully pondered the concepts.
- ☐ I've personally practiced the concepts.

1. Introduce the Session

• **Greet the group.** Explain that this session is devoted to interacting with Scripture. There is no video presentation, but a great opportunity to taste the fruit of God's Word.

• **Build the need.** *Ask:* "How would you like to leave this room with a simplified, better focused life? It can happen! We'll have an exciting time of study together today."

2. Divide into small groups.

• Place your members in units of three or four members each.

• Pray for everyone. Ask God's Spirit to guide each group into exciting discoveries.

3. Reviewing the Secrets

• Move quickly through the main points that have already been discussed. Some may have missed one or even both sessions. Review both sessions over a few minutes.

4. Pruning: What Have You Got to Lose?

Which category, or categories, describes how you are being pruned?

1—God is not pruning me at this point in time.

2—God is pruning me in priorities, and I'm exploring what is most important.

3—God is pruning me in purpose, and I'm rethinking my main focus.

4—God is pruning me in passion, and I'm enjoying certain activities less now.

5—I'm not at all certain, and I'd like to think about it some more.

Optional Session / Group Interaction

5. Discovering the Word: "Fruit" to " More Fruit"

1. *Read John 15:1-3 together and discuss the meaning of pruning.* From what you have learned already, how would you define what this term means in our lives as followers of Christ? *(God prunes us by working to remove every part of our lives that does not support the production of much fruit.)*

2. What is the difference between pruning and discipline? How are they similar? *(Discipline is the result of our disobedience—refusing to bear fruit—while pruning is the result of our doing what is right—God is preparing us to bear even more fruit. They are similar because God uses the same tools. Discipline and pruning feel the same to us.)*

3. When can we expect pruning to occur? How should that effect our feelings about it? Our response to it? *(It occurs when we are bearing fruit, so we should be encouraged and cooperate with God in pushing out the things in life that distract us from bearing fruit. If we expect God to work in us this way, we will feel much less pain when it occurs.)*

4. What are the three pruning principles? In which areas is God dealing with you, and what is the evidence? *(The exercise on the preceding page, #4, has already prepared your participants to think about this question. Allow them to share their answers together and to think about how they should respond this week.)*

5. Identify the single most important area in your life in which you could make changes to bear more fruit. How will you respond in the next few days? *(Again, allow group members to discuss this important and emotional question. Suggest sharing phone numbers and encouraging each other during the week.)*

6. Praying Together

Leave sufficient time for group prayer at the end of your session. Point out that pruning means that God loves us very much, and that the best is yet to come. Praise God and thank Him for the fruit that will be produced in the future by the members of this group as they participate with God in rechanneling their lives to be more and more useful. Ask for a breakthrough for each member during the week.

Homework: Question 5 above is the homework assignment. Ask each member to be ready to share their progress with the group at the next session.

SECRET #3:"MORE FRUIT" TO "MUCH FRUIT"

<table>
<tr><td>

Leader's Checklist

☐ I've fervently prayed for this session.

☐ I've thoroughly planned for this session.

☐ I've thoughtfully pondered the concepts.

☐ I've personally practiced the concepts.

</td></tr>
</table>

1. Introduce the Session

• **Launch the session.** We've made it together to the final portion of *Secrets of the Vine*. Highlight the main fruit-growing image from each of the first three units.

• **Introduce the material.** *Say:* "This has been a challenging course, hasn't it? If you're like me, you've found yourself looking deeply into your life and its purpose. Today we come to the most exciting, most joyful portion: it describes the future you can look forward to."

• **Build the need.** *Ask:* "What would your life be like if Jesus was truly your best friend? What would be the effect on you? We're going to find out today what it means to abide in Christ."

2. Play the Video (Course Workbook pages 54-57)

Allow 30 minutes for Dr. Wilkinson's video presentation.

Watch for the Big Idea: The greatest pleasure life offers is to abide in Christ. It brings abundant, lovely fruit and transforms us into all that the Lord longs for us to be.

When the video has concluded, ask your people to name the three wonderful truths about abiding. Make certain everyone received the main points, filled in their blanks, and so on.

3. Guide the Discussion.

Always take a moment for review, connecting the last session's insight to this week's insight.

1. What did you learn about abiding in Christ that you never knew before?

2. What would this group be like if every one of us abided deeply in Christ?

Divide the group into units of two or three. Direct them to the discussion questions on page 58 of the student workbook. Here are some comments to help you with each question.

Question 1.   It is important to review those key principles in defining the concept of abiding. Be sure everyone is clear. New believers struggle to abide because they often believe salvation is equivalent to abiding. They fail to understand that abiding is something they must choose to do.

Question 2.   Abiding is simply being connected to Christ, and work will not achieve it. We simply choose to pursue the relationship. It is encouraging to know we need not work harder or longer. But it is also true that we must spend more time with Christ to abide.

Question 3.   Have some fun and be creative. The directions given are clear; simply think of ways to abide with Christ in the course of life. Try to distill the best ones and distribute them to the group later.

Question 4.   As we abide in Christ, we begin to resemble Christ—it's the same way in any friendship. And as we are transformed to the image of Christ, we begin to pray about things He cares about. Also, He answers our prayers because He delights in our deep friendship.

Question 5.   The five points of this principle (pp. 31-32) are dynamic and moving. They help motivate us to bear fruit for Him. Knowing how deeply He loves us, we want to show our love for Him by bearing fruit. Bearing fruit is based in abiding, and abiding is life's richest joy.

Homework: Your assignment this week is quite simple. Can you guess what it is? Abide in Christ! No paperwork involved; simply dedicate extended time to Him this week, both privately and during periods when you can do so through the day. At the end of the week, reflect on the effect this has had on your life.

SECRET #3: "MORE FRUIT" TO "MUCH FRUIT"

Leader's Checklist
☐ I've fervently prayed for this session.
☐ I've thoroughly planned for this session.
☐ I've thoughtfully pondered the concepts.
☐ I've personally practiced the concepts.

1. Introduce the Session

• **Launch the session.** Ask for someone to share what it meant to them to abide in Christ over the last few days. Share a word of your own personal testimony.

• **Introduce the material.** *Say:* "We talk a lot about knowing God, but if we were honest we would admit that few of us know Him remotely as well as we would like. Abiding in Christ is the way to a deep, satisfying knowledge of Him."

• **Build the need.** *Ask:* "Have you ever thought, 'Someone show me how! I want to experience the presence of God, but I don't know where to begin. Could someone help me?' Most of us have thought that. Would you like answers? Listen carefully to our final video session."

2. Play the Video (Course Workbook pages 60-62)

Allow 30 minutes for Dr. Wilkinson's video presentation.

Watch for the Big Idea: God deeply, profoundly wants us to know and to love Him. Once we begin abiding, life becomes dynamic, exciting, and deeply fulfilling. It is truly the secret to life.

When the video has concluded, ask your group members to call out the various ways mentioned by Dr. Wilkinson that we can abide with Christ. Use the following two questions to begin your discussion.

3. Guide the Discussion.

Always take a moment for review, connecting the last session's insight to this week's insight.

1. Now that you've heard what it's like to abide in Christ, how do you feel about the relationship you've had in the past with Him? Why?

2. Why does abiding lead to more fruit-bearing?

Divide the group into units of two or three. Direct them to the discussion questions on page 63 of the student workbook. Here are some key insights to the questions.

Question 1. Everyone know what it's like to carry a passion for something—in romance, in a hobby, in a career. We call that glorying in something. Only by glorying in Christ can we lead a fulfilled, fruitful life. Group members should consider the "false glories" they pursue.

Question 2. Those who answer this question should use the details of their lives to demonstrate God's love for them. This can be a rich, gratifying exercise of thanksgiving.

Question 3. Many people feel intimidated by the spiritual disciplines, but those who pursue them would never give them up. Ask your members which ones they find most rewarding, and which they find most difficult. Point out what essential contribution is made by each discipline.

Question 4. In furthering our exploration of the last question, have each group member write out the names of the disciplines and assign a number rating to each, as specified in the question. Encourage them to share their victories, disappointments, and plans to master these disciplines.

Question 5. This is the final and central question of the entire course. Which basket are you in? What will it take for you to move into the next one? Ask each member to reveal their answer and share their plan for bearing more fruit for God in the future. Celebrate those who are excited about taking the next step.

Homework: This week, tune up your spiritual disciplines. Don't try to be perfect, but try to give each one a bit more attention and dedication than you have in the past. Ask God to give you a thirst for pursuing Him through these avenues for abiding. Look for more fruit immediately and in the future.

SECRET #3:"MORE FRUIT" TO "MUCH FRUIT"

Optional Session / Group Interaction

This should be the final session together.
Be sure to celebrate the wonderful things God has done in your group.

Leader's Checklist

☐ I've fervently prayed for this session.

☐ I've thoroughly planned for this session.

☐ I've thoughtfully pondered the concepts.

☐ I've personally practiced the concepts.

1. Introduce the Session

• **Greet the group.** Ask your group members to be prepared for a final week of breakthrough—one whose effects will last from here to eternity.

• **Build the need.** *Ask:* "Are you ready to go out and bear much fruit for God? What steps should you take? In this session we will prepare ourselves to be fruit-bearers from now until the day we stand before God to hear Him say, 'Well done!'"

2. Divide into small groups.

• Place your members in units of three or four members each.

• Pray for everyone. Ask God's Spirit to guide each group into exciting discoveries.

3. Reviewing the Secrets

• Review the four portions of the Secrets of the Vine. Give everyone an encouraging overview of just how far they have progressed.

4. Abiding: Are You in Christ?

Which category describes your current spiritual status?

1—I abide deeply in Christ every day.

2—I'd abide more deeply in Christ, but I'm walking in darkness.

3—I'd abide more deeply in Christ, but I feel anger toward someone.

4—I'd abide more deeply in Christ, but I don't faithfully keep His commandments.

5—I'm still not certain what it means to abide in Christ.

5. Discovering the Word: "More Fruit" to "Much Fruit"

Turn to John 15:4-5, 7, 9-11. Discuss the following questions, using the hints in parentheses.

1. Give your best definition of what it means to abide in Christ. Why is this so often difficult for Christians to do? (*Abiding is remaining in the presence of Christ by intention, and experiencing deep fellowship with Him consistently. Ignorance, sin, and lack of commitment are among the many reasons we fail to abide in Christ.*)

2. Abiding is something we do by choice. What are some obstacle in choosing to abide in Christ? (*Priorities, time, our lack of love for Him, our lack of understanding of how to abide in Christ, and the presence of sin in our lives are some of the obstacles.*)

3. Name the five spiritual disciplines described in this course. Which are the most rewarding for you? Which are the most difficult? (*Devotions, Scripture, prayer, worship, journaling*)

4. It will take a great deal of time to master all of the five disciplines. Which do you plan to begin with, and why? (*Encourage your group members not to feel intimidated by these five demanding pursuits, but to gradually grow in each of them, concentrating on certain ones.*)

5. How will your life change in the future as a result of this course? What will you do to be certain you keep your commitment to bearing more fruit? (*Leave the most time of all for your group to answer this question and celebrate the breakthroughs they've made. Make plans to meet in the future and see how everyone is progressing. Create a simple checklist for one year from now.*)

6. Praying Together

Since this is your final session together, spend much of your time in prayers of praise and worship. You might also hold a time of commitment, allowing people to stand or identify themselves in some way if they are making decisions to make major changes in their lives. Encourage and applaud those decisions. Close your time together with singing and sharing about the great things God has done in your group, and the wonderful fruit you will each bear in the future as you serve Him with joy and gladness.